FUN
WITH STRING FIGURES

W. W. ROUSE BALL

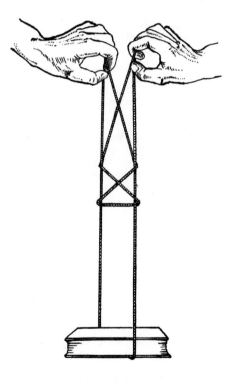

DOVER PUBLICATIONS, INC.

NEW YORK

This Dover edition, first published in 1971, is an
unabridged republication of the third edition of
the work first published by W. Heffer & Sons, Ltd.,
Cambridge, England, in 1920, under the title *An
Introduction to String Figures*. An Introductory
Note and Supplement have been added to the
Dover edition.

International Standard Book Number: 0-486-22809-6
Library of Congress Catalog Card Number: 76-173664

Manufactured in the United States of America
Dover Publications, Inc.
180 Varick Street
New York, N. Y. 10014

Prefatory Note

THE making of String Figures is a game common among primitive people. Its study by men of science is a recent development; their researches have, however, already justified its description as a hobby, pleasing to most people and readily mastered. The following pages contain a lecture which I gave in 1920 at the Royal Institution, London, on these figures and their history (Proceedings, Vol. xxiii. pp. 77–110); to it I have appended full directions for the construction of several easy typical designs, arranged roughly in order of difficulty, and, for those who wish to go further, lists of additional patterns and references. The only expense necessary to anyone who takes up the pastime is the acquisition of a piece of good string some seven feet long; with that and this booklet to aid him, he will have at his command an amusement that may occupy many a vacant hour.

I have avoided as far as is practicable the use of technical terms, but for the convenience of those who consult other works I have added to the index of this, the third edition, a glossary of terms in common use.

W. W. ROUSE BALL

Trinity College, Cambridge.

Contents

Introductory Note to the
Dover Edition

BECAUSE of the importance of certain key movements and openings in making the string figures in this book, a supplement has been added on pages 67-72 to provide additional illustrations and instructions for the following: the First Position, Openings A and B, the Navaho Opening, and Navahoing a Loop.

FUN
WITH STRING FIGURES

NOTE : *The figures in the text are drawn as seen by the Operator.*

A Lecture on String Figures

———

I HAVE chosen as the subject for this Lecture *String Figures*, which I present to you as a world-wide amusement of primitive man, and as being in themselves interesting to most people. In the course of the evening you will see how such figures are actually made, but before coming to that I must say something about their nature and history.   I hope you will bear with me if I introduce them to you in my own way.

A string figure is usually made by taking a piece of good flexible string, such as macrami thread, about six-and-a-half feet long, knotting the ends so as to make it into a closed loop, and then weaving or twisting this loop on the fingers so as to produce a pleasing design.

Having taken up the loop of string in some defined way, the subsequent weaving may be effected either with the aid of another operator, each player in turn taking the string from the other, or by the single player making a series of movements, such as dropping a loop from one finger, transferring a loop from one finger to another, picking up a string with one finger and then returning the finger to its original position carrying the string with it, and so on ; unless I state the contrary it is to be assumed that it is with figures made in the second way that I am concerned to-night.   In general, after each step, the hands are separated so as to make the string tight ; and normally the hands are held upright with the fingers pointing upwards and the palms approximately facing one another.   [These movements were illustrated by the formation of one or two string figures.] Nothing more is required in most constructions, though many other small movements, notably slight rotations of the wrists, while not necessary, give neatness of manipulation and add to the effectiveness of the display.

These figures, when shown to a few spectators in a room, always prove, as far as my experience goes, interesting alike to young and old; but their attractiveness, their fascination I might almost say, is not permanent unless people can be induced to construct them for themselves. I can hardly propose—and that is a difficulty inherent in lecturing on the subject —I can hardly propose that for the first time, now and here, without individual help, you should make the designs you will see later. To enjoy the occupation, however, you must be able to make them, and, bold though I may seem, I venture to assert that if once you acquire this knowledge you will find pleasure in applying it.

It is a truism, and in fact a truth as well, that all sensible people have hobbies. I am not alone in finding that collecting string figures is an agreeable hobby, and it may be added a very cheap one, while friends who have learnt how to make them tell me that in convalescence and during tedious journeys the amusement has helped to while away many a long hour; moreover the figures are easy to weave, they have a history, and they are capable of numerous varieties. Thus even in England the game may prove well worth the time spent in learning to play it; and admittedly to the very few who travel among aborigines it may sometimes be of real service.

It would be absurd to talk about string figures if you do not know what they are; so before I go any further let me show you what is meant by the term. These figures may be divided into three classes, a, β, γ, according as (a) the production of a design, or (β) the illustration of some action or story, or (γ) the creation of a surprise effect is the object desired; it will be desirable to begin by giving one or two examples of each class.

The designs reproduced in figures 1 and 2 are well-known froms which will serve as illustrations of figures in Class A. Like all those given in this booklet they are drawn as seen by the person who makes them.

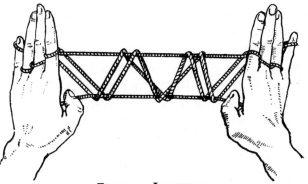

FIGURE 1—LIGHTNING.

The first of them, a zig-zag pattern, termed *Lightning*, is due to the Navaho Indians who live in the far West, on the Mexican border of Arizona, where the customs of the Red Man have not yet been destroyed by civilization and law. [The figure as shown by the Lecturer was made by successive movements, as set out in the next paragraph.] The construction is simple, and no digital skill is involved. You see the final result appears suddenly, almost dramatically, and I regard this as an excellent feature of it. Observe also that the production of the figure is rapid. Timing myself, I find I take about six seconds to make it. I think quickness, which comes easily as soon as one knows the moves, adds finish to the working and is worth cultivating.

In making the figure, this is what I did. *First*, I put the string in the form of a figure of eight, one oval (preferably small) lying away from me, and the other towards me, and the strings crossing in the middle of the figure ; I then put my index-fingers down into the far oval, and my thumbs down into the near oval ; next I separated the hands and then turned them up into their normal position with the thumbs and fingers well spread out, thus causing the strings of the loops on the thumbs and index-fingers to cross one another : this is called the *Navaho Opening*. *Second*, I bent each thumb away from me over two strings, and with its back picked up from below the next string (i.e. in the language expounded later, the ulnar index string), and, as usually follows and is assumed to be the case unless the contrary is stated, returned the thumbs to their former positions. *Third*, I bent each mid-finger towards me over one string, and with its back picked up from below the next string. *Fourth*, I bent each ring-finger towards me over one string, and with its back picked up from below the next string. *Fifth*, I bent each little-finger towards me over one string, and with its back picked up from below the next string. *Sixth*, I moved my thumbs away from me, and placed their tips in the spaces by the little-fingers, their fronts resting on the near little-finger string ; this released the thumb loops. *Lastly*, I threw the loops thus released over the other strings, and at the same time with the thumbs pressed down the near little-finger string sharply and as far as possible, and the figure flashed out.

The description is lengthy, but in my opinion it is not desirable to labour at making this extremely concise. As is the case in many of these figures, the resulting pattern is shown stretched or hung on parallel horizontal strings, and to present it effectively it is desirable to keep these strings widely separated. To those who know something of these figures the construction is easy, and a boy of eight or nine, if taught practically, can learn it in a few minutes; none the less, a novice of more mature years will be well advised to begin with even simpler forms, some of which are given below in the addendum.

The next diagram is of a design, known as a *Tent Flap* or

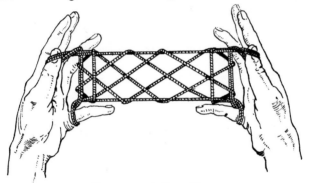

FIGURE 2—A TENT FLAP.

Door, due to the Apache Red Indians. [The figure as shown by the Lecturer was made as set out below on page 31.] The tribe is now almost extinct, but the figure is familiar to various Indians, who are said to have originally got it from Apaches living on the Reservation Lands maintained by the United States Government. This also is a figure in Class A.

The two designs, represented in figures 3 and 4, will serve as examples of figures in Class B. The first of them is supposed to represent a *Man Climbing a Tree*, his arms and feet (or perhaps his tree-band and feet) clasping the tree trunk. It is derived from the Blacks in Queensland; since only a drawing of the design was brought away, it is impossible to be certain how it was made by the aborigines, but the construction I am about to employ has been suggested, and is probably correct, since

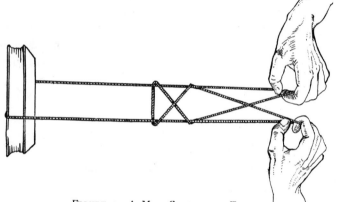

FIGURE 3—A MAN CLIMBING A TREE.

it is simple and involves no unusual actions. [The figure as shown by the Lecturer was made as set out on page 52.] In the figure thus obtained (which is here drawn as seen sideways) I pull with my index-fingers, and then the part which represents the man moves up the part which represents the tree trunk. Such motion is characteristic of figures of this kind; hence such results are often used as a framework for stories—two warriors fighting, a hammock breaking and its occupant falling out, and so on.

String Illustrations of Stories may be employed as examples of Class B. The well-known representation of the *Yam Theft* will serve as a specimen. [The construction as shown by the Lecturer was made as set out below on page 49, the final form being shown in the accompanying diagram.] You can tell the story much as you like. In one version of it the thumb loop represents the owner of a yam patch. He is supposed to be asleep. The loops successively taken up from the dorsal string and put on the fingers represent

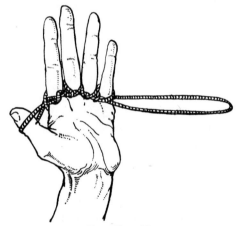

FIGURE 4—THE YAM THIEF.

the yams dug up by a thief, and tied up in bags ready for carrying off. The loop coming off the thumb represents the owner waking and going to see what is the matter. He looks down the back of the hand, sees the yams collected for removal, notices that the dorsal string holds them tight, and looks about for the thief. The thief, who may be represented by a loop on the pendant palmar string, coming back for his booty, sees the owner, whereupon (pulling that string) he disappears with all the yams.   There is a well known British specimen of such a string story which deals with the misadventures of a thief who stole some tallow candles.

There is yet a third class, which I call Class Γ, of string figures to which primitive man is very partial ; these are string paradoxes, where the unexpected happens.   Take this as an example.   Here is a loop of string, held for convenience by my left hand high up.   Obviously if I twist my right hand round one string of the loop and pull with the left hand, the right hand will be caught.   If I give the right hand a twist round the other string of the loop, it is generally still more firmly caught.   The problem is to give this additional twist so that the string runs free when the left hand is pulled.   This can easily be effected by what is known in certain South Pacific Isles as the *Lizard Twist*.   [This was shown and explained.] There is no trickery ; the movements are simple, yet I predict that few people, even if they have seen the twist, will succeed when they first attempt to make it.   String paradoxes or puzzles of this kind are widely known, and are generally amusing.   To show them, to be shown them, and above all to show pleasure in them, often lead to friendly intercourse with primitive folk, but they are different in kind from the figures about which I wish to talk.   I put them, then, on one side as not relevant to my subject to-night, and come back to the formation as practised to-day of string designs in classes α and β.

The study of string figures is new, and its history a short one.   I may dispose of the story prior to 1902 very briefly. From about the middle of the nineteenth century onwards we find occasional notices by travellers in wild countries of the fact that the natives made, with a piece of string, forms different from and far more elaborate than the Cat's Cradle of our nurseries, but (with the exception of two examples described in France in 1888 and two in America in 1900) no details were given of how they were constructed, and in only a few cases near the end of the century were drawings kept of the patterns produced. There are more accounts of the Cat's Cradle familiar to children in England; indeed they stretch back to the eighteenth century, for there is an allusion to it in English literature as long ago as 1768, and Charles Lamb refers to it as played at Christ's Hospital in his school-days. It is, however, a dull amusement, producing, as usually presented, merely four or five designs of little interest; here, too, before the present century, no description was available which would enable anyone previously ignorant of the Cradle to make it. Outside Britain, in the nineteenth century it was known in Northern Europe, and travellers in Victorian times mention it as practised in Korea, China, and the Asiatic Isles

We may say that before 1902 the whole matter of string figures was regarded as a pastime of children and savages, hardly worth mention and not worth consideration. To-day, when serious attention is given to folk-lore and the histories of games, such things are looked at from a different stand-point. The study of string figures came about in this way. In 1898, Rivers and Haddon organised an anthropological expedition to the Torres Straits, and, among other things, they brought back information about string patterns there current, together with some thirty examples. Some of these designs were made to the chanting of sing-songs, some were connected with tribal stories, and some were devised as amusements, but everything suggested that here was a custom worth investigation.

This conclusion showed the need of having an unambiguous nomenclature which would allow anyone acquainted with it to describe a string figure in such a way as to permit of its reproduction by an intelligent reader. The terms introduced are taken from anatomy, and there is nothing recondite about them, but it is necessary to know them if you want to understand recent writers on the subject. Here they are :—

The part of a string which lies across the palm of the hand is described as *palmar*, the part lying across the back of the hand as *dorsal*.

Anything on the thumb side of the hand is called *radial*, anything on the little-finger side is called *ulnar*. Since a string passing round a finger or fingers forms a loop, each such loop is composed of a radial string, and an ulnar string.

Of two strings or loops on the same finger, the one nearer the palm of the hand is called *proximal*, and the one nearer the finger tip is called *distal*.

These six adjectives, palmar and dorsal, radial and ulnar, proximal and distal, together with the names of the parts of the hands, fingers, wrists, etc., enable us to state exactly the relative place of every string in a figure held on the hands.

This nomenclature is framed so as to define the position of strings on a hand by reference to the hand, and not by terms like near and far, lower and upper, which may mean quite different things according as to how it is held. At the same time, if the hands are held upright, and with the palms facing each other, which I regard as their normal position, we may conveniently use *near* and *far* instead of radial and ulnar, and *lower* and *upper* instead of proximal and distal.   It is, however, well to make it a rule that this every-day language is used only when the hands are in their normal position or when there can be no doubt as to the meaning; when there is no ambiguity I prefer to employ these ordinary words rather than the technical terms.

Precision of language, which was necessary if the subject was to be treated scientifically, was introduced only in 1902. Subsequent research has strengthened the interest taken in string figures, and in anthropological expeditions to-day they are among the matters on which information is sought.   In particular Haddon has continued to stimulate enquiry, and to him we owe several of the patterns discovered.   It is not too much to say that he is the creator of the science, and to his enthusiasm many owe their introduction to it.

The Americans took up the investigation warmly, and in Philadelphia a valuable collection of drawings of string figures has been formed which will permanently preserve the patterns discovered. The results of the earlier work in America are embodied in a handsome volume published in New York in 1906, containing full descriptions of about a hundred string figures, chiefly collected in North America and New Guinea, though with some examples from Africa, the Philippines, and other scattered localities.   In it also are given drawings of more than another hundred finished patterns from Oceania and Queensland. Unfortunately Mrs. Jayne, to whose liberality and initiative the book was due, died shortly after its publication.

Further examples from places where the amusement was already known to exist, and collections from Africa and India, have since been issued, and show that the construction of string figures is widely practised where primitive man is still found. Examples also have been reported from South America, but as yet this immense area is an almost unworked field, the only well-known South American instance being a *Mosquito* or *Fly*—an example of Class B. [The figure as shown by the Lecturer was made as set out below on page 45.] The insect with its body and wings appears between the hands. Of course in such a position the natural thing is to try to squash it. To do this you clap your hands sharply together, then drawing them apart quickly and at the same time releasing the little-fingers, you will find that here, as usually happens in life, you have failed, and the fly has gone.

In 1911 K. Haddon published in London an excellent account, employing the customary technical terms, of several results. Later, in 1914, P. Hambruch printed at Hamburg a long memoir on the subject, with special regard to the patterns found at Nauru in Micronesia, the home of some of the most skilful native exponents of the art, and then a German possession. Of course the outbreak of war in 1914 put a stop to researches of this kind, as of so many others[1]. Hence, up to to-day (1920), the serious study of the subject covers only twelve years—namely, from 1902 to 1914—and as yet few save specialists know much about it; but materials increase rapidly, and the number of recorded specimens, which in 1902 was less than fifty, already runs to some hundreds.

[1] Before the end of the war, work on the subject had recommenced; and in particular I note R. H. Compton's interesting paper in the Journal of the Royal Anthropological Institute, vol. 49 (printed subsequently to the delivery of my Lecture), giving an account and the workings of 25 figures, including *The Caterpillar*, *The Ebbing Tide*, and *The Porker*, collected by him from Lifu and New Caledonia. The workings of these three figures are given below.

I may sum up the result of the work of these twelve years by saying that the evidence does not justify us in asserting dogmatically that all primitive people play and always have played at making string figures ; but we may say that the game was at one time common among a large number of them. The formation of these designs is natural, for there are not many sedentary occupations open to uncivilized man during his long leisure hours, and to toy with a piece of string is an obvious recreation[1]. What, however, is striking, is the immense variety of well-defined patterns already discovered, and their distribution in different parts of the world.

The search for and collection of designs was begun just in time. The development of such branches of anthropology as are concerned with the amusements of primitive man is a tragic story. Put on a scientific basis only at the extreme close of the nineteenth century, already the materials for research are fast disappearing. Everywhere and ever more eagerly the white man seeks for new fields to explore, and his intercourse with aboriginals remorselessly destroys recreations such as those here described; under his influence everything tends to become uniform and colourless. Ethnologists tell us that these primitive games are now being discarded by adults, and survive only among the children; it would really seem that their continuance is almost incompatible with civilization as we know it, and I suspect that this is why, until recently, when Cat's Cradle was imported from Asia, there were in European literature, covering centuries of cultured life, no allusions to string figures.

[1] A correspondent, writing to me from the Gold Coast in 1921 on figures found there, informed me that besides their normal use for illustrating stories or indicating objects a few forms (thrown, so to speak, at the spectator) are sometimes employed as signs of good-humoured abuse—an interesting local development.

Among existing aborigines, it is usually the women who
teach the pastime to the children, and in most cases now-a-days
the lads and men, though familiar with the methods used, do
not of their own accord make designs in the presence of
strangers.   Hence the amusement may easily escape the attention of travellers ; no doubt, also, many of these would
take in no interest in such figures even if they saw them.   Moreover, in wild countries the natives are shy, and think that the
white man will laugh at these simple games ; thus an exhibition
is not made unless encouraged by sympathetic advances, but
if patterns are shown no secret is made about the method of
construction, which is not treated as a tribal secret.   To this
open revelation of methods of weaving there is one reported
exception mentioned by F. Boas, and referred to later.   When
figures are displayed, it does not follow that it is easy to take
down or follow the rapid sequence of moves made by the
operator, so the collection of records may involve a good deal
of gentle diplomacy.

I can give an illustration of this reluctance to show
figures unless they are asked for.   A few years ago a traveller,
near the Victoria Falls in Africa, met a high official of the
Government, and, enquiring about various customs of the
natives, asked if any string games were known in that part of
the country.   The officer said, " No " ;   he had never heard
of them, he had lived for years among these people, had
constantly seen them at work and at play, and was confident
that nothing of the kind could exist without his knowledge.
After their talk the visitor strolled to where the police escort
waited, and taking out of his pocket a piece of string (without
which to-day no self-respecting anthropologist ought to travel),

distrust a missionary, a prospector, and a trader; but a stranger, who exhibits what may well be taken to be one of the innocent games of his own people, offers credentials to which a friendly response is, as far as experience goes, invariably made. Who, indeed, would attribute evil intentions to one who comes armed only with a piece of string, and seems chiefly interested in amusements similar to those familiar to the onlookers in their childhood? This is not a matter of mere conjecture. I know of more than one definite instance where cordial relations were thus immediately established.

Of course from the beginning of the study of these figures the question arose of their possible relation to historical and religious traditions. Until now, however, with the exception of a few isolated facts, no evidence of such connection has been found. Indeed the only traces of it so far recorded are that in New Zealand the forms are associated with mythical heroes and the invention of the game is attributed to Maui, the first man; that various designs common to many of the Polynesians are often made to the accompaniment of ancient chants; that the Eskimo, too, have songs connected with particular patterns, have a prejudice against boys playing the game for fear it should lead to their getting entangled with harpoon lines, and hold that such figures, if made at all should be constructed in the autumn so as to entangle the sun in the string and delay the advent of the long winter night. Further, Boas asserts that among the natives of Vancouver Island the form known as " Threading a Closed Loop " is used instead of a password by members of a certain secret society to recognise fellow-members. These facts, interesting though they be, do not come to much, and it would seem that as yet there is no substantial evidence that the construction of string figures is other than a recreation. I say " as yet," for new discoveries may at any time alter our views on this question.

Now let me put aside these historical questions, and consider the patterns actually made and their making. In opening the subject I remarked that for constructing string figures two methods are commonly applied ; these are known respectively as the *Asiatic* and the *Oceanic*. In the former, two players are required, of whom one at each move takes the string from the other ; in the latter, normally, only one player is required, who weaves the pattern with his fingers, using, if need be, his feet and teeth to assist him.

The Asiatic method lends itself to many varieties, but as far as I am aware these have not been developed, and broadly speaking this method is known to us almost only in the classical form, common in the English nursery, of Cat's Cradle. This form occurs in Korea, Japan, the Asiatic Islands, China, and Northern Europe, and the result is a figure of Class A. The weaving begins by the first player twisting the string round the four fingers of each hand, so as to make two dorsal strings and one palmar string ; next picking up the string lying on the palm of each hand with the back of the mid-finger of the other hand, he draws the hands apart. In England, the four fundamental figures, which can be made in succession, are termed the cradle, a snuffer-tray, cat's-eye, and fish-in-a-dish. These are shown in the diagram given below on page 41; the method of construction is widely known, see below, p. 40 *et seq*, and I need not display it here. Another figure, called a pound of candles, is usually (though unnecessarily) interpolated: a few other designs and an arrangement for a See-Sawing movement can also be

introduced. That is all. In Korea the four fundamental
figures are designated a hearse, a chess-board, a cow's-eye, a
rice-pestle, and the interpolated figure chop-sticks. In other
places other names are given.

I need not describe Cat's Cradle further. As usually
played, it leads only to a fixed sequence of four or five forms ;
there are three or four standard moves, and by using these in
various orders other forms can be obtained. No skill is
required, and probably to-day ethnologists are the only people
of mature age who concern themselves with it. It is believed to
have had its origin in Eastern Asia, and to have been thence
conveyed to Northern Europe, perhaps by tea traders. A map
of the localities in which it is practised shows a band of marks
along the east and north of Asia and the north of Europe
From England, with its unceasing output of emigrants,
missionaries, and venturers, it has probably been carried to
other localities, but I do not think it is common outside the
places I have named.

Oceanic examples of Classes A and B are more interesting
and far more widely spread. They occur among the Eskimo,
and the natives in America (North and South), Oceania, Australasia, Africa, and India, though the last-named country, as we
might expect from its ancient civilization, has not given us
many designs. In this form there is almost invariably only
one player. The figures produced are numerous, and many of
them can be made, and are made, in more than one way. In
this country only one Oceanic construction, known as the
Leashing of Lochiel's Dogs, has been discovered. [The figure
as shown by the Lecturer was made as set out below on
page 33.] This, in some places termed *Crow's Feet*, is the most

widely distributed of string designs as yet catalogued. It
may be indigenous in Great Britain, but in a sea-surrounded

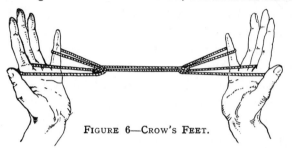

FIGURE 6—CROW'S FEET.

land like this, having ship communication with all parts of
the world, it seems more likely that it is an importation.

Recently I came across an instance of how such figures may
be introduced here   A friend of mine, then living at an inland
town, showed me a well-known figure, sometimes called a
Fishing Net, sometimes *Quadruple Diamonds*, which has been

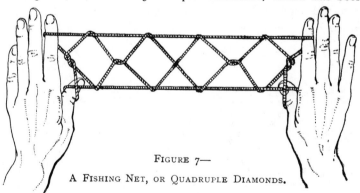

FIGURE 7—

A FISHING NET, OR QUADRUPLE DIAMONDS.

found in Africa, Oceania, and America, but was said to be un-
known in Europe. [The figure as shown by the Lecturer was
made as set out below on page 36.] This figure he had learnt

here in boyhood, and therefore supposed it to be an English production. On enquiry we found that his nurse had taught it to him, and as a result of further talk it seemed that she had got it from a sailor to whom she had been engaged to be married; the conclusion that the latter had learnt it in the course of his voyages seems a safe one. The figure in question is typical of the numerous patterns made of diamond-shaped lozenges strung between two parallel strings, arranged either in single rows (of one or two or more, as the case may be) or in the form of rows side by side as in figure 2, see above, page 5.

A remarkable feature in the Oceanic examples is that a large number of the figures begin in one way. In this the tips of the thumbs and little-fingers of each hand are put together, and then from below into the loop of string ; next the digits are separated, and the hands drawn apart (this is called the *First Position*); and, lastly, the palmar loop on each hand is picked up by the back of the index-finger of the other hand : this is known as *Opening A* or *B*. In the accompanying diagram

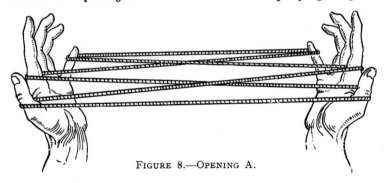

FIGURE 8.—OPENING A.

the loops on the little-fingers are drawn as being on the tips of the fingers: this is done to make the diagram clearer, but in

working it is more usual to keep that loop near the base
of the little-fingers.   The fact that such a normal (and
not very obvious) opening exists all over the world suggests
either that the game was played by the ancestors of the existing
races before they were widely dispersed, or that in the long
series of past generations there has been more occasional intercourse between natives of distant localities than was formerly
suspected, and of course a single stray voyager, whether travel-
ling on his own initiative or driven from home by some un-
happy chance, might serve to carry with him the methods of
making such figures traditional among his own folk.   Either
view implies a long history, perhaps extending over thousands
of years.

   In *Opening A* the left palmar string is taken up before the
right palmar string.   If the right palmar string is taken up by the
left index finger before the left palmar string is taken up by the
right index finger we obtain *Opening B*.   In most Oceanic
figures it is immaterial whether we begin with Opening A or
Opening B.

   There is also another movement, known as *Navahoing*,
which occurs in the construction of many figures.   This is
when we have on a finger two loops, one proximal and the
other distal, and the proximal loop is pulled over the distal
loop, then over the tip of the finger, and then dropped on the
palmar side of the hand.   This movement is not uncommon.
It was first discovered among the Navaho Indians : hence it
is called *Navahoing the Loop*.

   And now having talked at large about the subject, I want
to spend the remaining time in showing you a few of the more
interesting of these Oceanic figures.   [Some figures illustrative

of different openings and actions were then shown, and their histories briefly given.]   I had originally intended to conclude by showing lantern slides of natives displaying various figures; but I can do better, for Mrs. Rishbeth, whose adventurous travels among aborigines are well known, has kindly consented to come to London to show us various examples, most of which have never before been exhibited in public.   [Mrs. Rishbeth then showed fourteen examples of string figures.]

In selecting these constructions as the subject of this Lecture I have been venturesome, but I plead guilty to liking to wander in the outlying fields of science, and, as I have found pleasure in String Figures and their history, I hoped that others might do the same.

Addendum

String designs have little interest except to those who know how to make them. Their construction however is not a difficult operation, and to smooth the path of would-be learners I add these notes on figures I made in the Lecture, together with a few other typical ones. When figures are made by different peoples there are often slight differences in the workings, and in such cases I select whichever construction I consider simplest ; in my opinion, there is no objection to varying petty details. When once learnt, all string figures are easy, and with the exception of Cat's Cradle, the Ebbing Tide, and the Porker, none of those here described should, when mastered, take more than a few seconds to construct. To any who may find my language ambiguous, I may say that in my directions the words *near, far, above,* and *below,* may, if it be thought clearer, be replaced by the words *radial, ulnar, distal,* and *proximal,* respectively. In the following descriptions, a knowledge of the First Position and of Opening A (see above, page 20), of the Navaho Opening (see page 4), and of the Navahoing Movement (see page 21) is assumed.

The operations are facilitated if the string is smooth, flexible, and not very thin: crochetted doubled silk is almost ideal. I venture to add that generally if, in the weaving, a mistake is made, or a loop accidentally dropped, it is well not to try to correct the error, but to start again from the beginning. Also when two loops are on one digit, it is desirable to keep each clear of the other.

I have selected these examples in nearly equal numbers from the two standard classes, and placed those in each class roughly in order of difficulty ; I advise the novice to mix his diet, and not to learn all those in one class before he begins to make those in the other.

For the benefit of any reader who has mastered the constructions here presented and wishes to go further I have, at the end of each class, mentioned a few additional figures in it, and in my notes on Authorities, have stated where descriptions of them can be found.

CLASS A.   Of figures in Class A, I choose the following as being interesting and easy.—a *Fish Spear*, an *Outrigged Canoe*, a *Moth*, a *Frame-work for a Hut*, the *Batoka Gorge*, *Carrying Wood*, a *Tent Flap*, *Crow's Feet*, *Lightning*, *Little Fishes*, the *Veiled Sun*, a *Fishing Net*, a *Butterfly*, the *Laia Fruit*, and *Cat's Cradle*.

1. *A FISH SPEAR* (Class A).   This is one of the simplest of String Figures, and its construction requires no skill.   It is widely distributed, being found in New Guinea and the adjoining regions, and along the Western side of North America. The result is said to represent a three-pronged spear, the handle being held by the right index and the ends of the three prongs resting on the left hand.   In British Columbia the figure is known as *Pitching a Tent*, the six strings from the left hand being taken to represent a frame work of six poles tied together at their tops.

It is made thus :—*First*, Take up the string in the form of the First Position.   *Second*, With the back of the right index pick up, from below, the string which lies across the palm of the left hand, give it a couple of twists by rotating the right index, and return. *Third*, Pass the left index through the loop on the right index, then with its back pick up, from below, the string which lies across the palm of the right hand, and return.

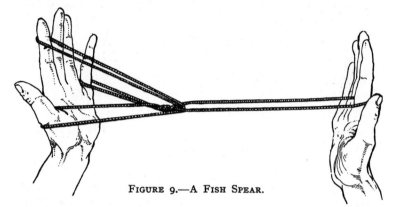

FIGURE 9.—A FISH SPEAR.

Lastly, Release the right thumb and little-finger, and extend, that is, draw the hands apart as far as practicable into their normal position.

The working may be summarised thus:—Opening A, except that the right index, after picking up the left palmar string, gives it two twists. Release right thumb and little-finger, and extend.

2. *AN OUTRIGGED CANOE* (Class A). This also is very easy to construct, though it is uninteresting except as an introduction to the subject. It comes to us from New Caledonia.

It is made thus:—*First*, Opening A. *Second*, Bend each thumb away from you over two strings, pick up on its back the far index string, and return. *Third*, Navaho the loops on the thumbs. *Lastly*, Release the little-fingers, and extend. For diagram see over-page.

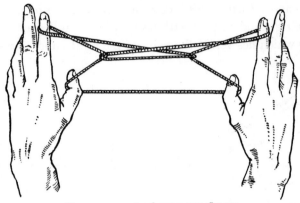

FIGURE 10.—AN OUTRIGGED CANOE.

3. *A MOTH* (Class A).   This is interesting as an example
of a Zulu construction; it was discovered in 1905.   The full
length of the string is not needed, and the figure is best presented by using the string doubled.   The construction is easy,
and follows typical lines.

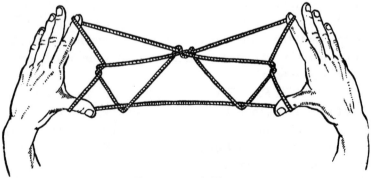

FIGURE 11.—A MOTH.

It is made thus:—*First*, Opening A. *Second*, Release the
thumbs. *Third*, Pass each thumb over both strings of the

index loop, and with its back pick up, from below, the near little-finger string. *Fourth*, Release the little-fingers. *Fifth*, Pass each thumb over one string, and with its back pick up, from below, the near index string. *Sixth*, Navaho the thumb strings and extend. *Lastly*, Put each index finger downwards into the loop hung on the string running from the far side of the thumb to the near side of the index-finger, thus allowing the existing index loops to slip off; extend, the fingers pointing downwards. This shows the insect with its wings outspread.

Some of the Zulus describe the resulting figure as a pair of spectacles, and putting it up to the face look through two of the holes.

4 *A FRAME WORK FOR A HUT* (Class A). This figure is supposed to represent eight poles tied together at their tops, forming a frame-work for a tent or hut.   If the design is turned upside down it might well represent a *Parachute*.

In Central Africa, it is constructed thus:—*First*, Holding the left hand horizontal, pointing to the right, and palm downwards place the string on it in the First Position, giving a long loop hanging down in front of the hand.   *Second*, With the right thumb and index take up the string lying on the back of the left thumb, pull it over the back of that hand, and let it hang in a short loop on the far side of the hand.   *Third*, Pull the short loop through the long one, and loop it over the left index : draw tight, and raise the left hand into its normal position.   *Fourth*, With the right thumb and index, pick up the string which is on the near side of the left little-finger, taking hold of it as close to the little-finger as possible, pull it out, and loop it over the left thumb.   *Lastly*, With the right thumb and index take hold of that string on the back of the hand which runs across the knuckles, pull it over the left fingers on to the front of the hand, and draw it away from the left hand : this movement can be assisted by working the left hand.

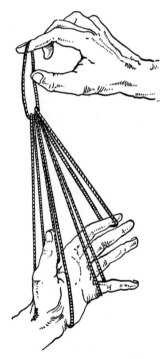

FIGURE 12—A FRAME WORK FOR A HUT.

Among the Red Indians a similar figure called a *Hogan* is made by a different process, thus :—*First*, Put the left index and mid-finger through the loop, a short piece of string resting across the back of the hand and a long loop hanging down in front. *Second,* Put the right index, from the near side, under the near string between the left index and mid-finger, over the cross string at the back of the hand, and with its tip pick up the cross string, and return ; extend, and release the right index. *Third,* Put the right hand from the near side under the near hanging string into the pendant loop, and then with the right thumb and index take hold of the two strings between the left index and mid-finger, return through the pendant loop, and extend; release the right hand. *Fourth,* Bend the left thumb from you, and with its back pick up below the knot the near index string; bend the left little-finger towards you, and with its back pick up below the knot the far mid-finger string. *Lastly,* With the right thumb and index pick up that string on the left palm which goes across and over the two other strings on that palm ; pull with the right hand, and the figure is formed.

5. *THE BATOKA GORGE* (Class A) ; for diagram, see page 15, figure 5. In my Lecture I mentioned and showed this figure, and I have nothing to add to what I there said. It is interesting from the way in which it was discovered, and as being one of the few recorded attempts to represent geographical features by a string pattern. The construction is peculiar to the natives near the Victoria Falls in Africa.

It is made thus :—*First,* Hold the right hand horizontal, pointing away from you and with its palm facing downwards; rest the string on the right wrist so that two equal loops hang freely down, one on its radial side, the other on its ulnar side. *Second,* Pass the left hand from left to right through both loops, and bring both hands into their normal positions. *Third,* Bend each little-finger towards you, and with its back pick up both the strings which cross each other in the centre of the figure. *Fourth,* Throw the near wrist string away from you over both hands to their far side. *Fifth,* Bend each thumb away from you, and with its back pick up the corresponding oblique near little-finger string. *Lastly,* Take each far wrist string and (keeping the other strings unaltered in position) pass it over the hand to the near side of the wrist. Extend the hands, and the figure, representing a bird's-eye view of the zig-zag course of the river through the gorge, will appear.

6. *CARRYING WOOD* (Class A). This is a figure made by Mexican Indians. The construction is simple, and the result pleasing. The result is supposed to show poles lying on a sledge.

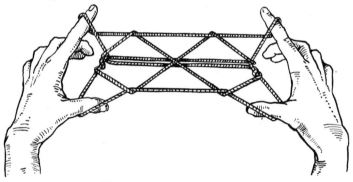

FIGURE 13.—CARRYING WOOD.

It is made thus :—*First,* Opening A. *Second,* Pass the thumb and index-finger of each hand above the index loop, and put them, from below, into the little-finger loop. Release the little-finger, thus transferring the little-finger loop to the thumb and index-finger. *Third,* Navaho the loops on the thumbs and index-fingers, but keep the strings hanging loose. There is now a string hanging in front of the figure and running straight across it. *Lastly*, Put each thumb away from you over this cross string, let the loops on each thumb slip off, and extend with the thumbs pointing away from you and the palms facing outwards.

7. *A TENT FLAP* (Class A); for diagram, see page 5, figure 2. I have in my Lecture mentioned and delineated this figure, and I need not here repeat what is there set out. The design is familiar to most of the Mexican Indians, who attribute its origin to the Apaches, a tribe now almost extinct. The result shows a pretty piece of string network which looks like a *Hurdle*, but is said to have been intended to represent the flap, or perhaps lacing, covering the opening to a tent; it has alternative descriptive names, such as a *Poncho*, a *Sling*, a *Net*, and so on.

There is a touch of romance in the story of its discovery. In September, 1904, Haddon, on his way to England, stopping one night at Philadelphia with H. H. Furness, expressed to Mrs. Jayne, the daughter of his host, his regret that he had no time to go to the St. Louis Exposition, where he understood he might meet some Mexican Indians whose tribal customs had not been investigated, and the talk drifted on to String Figures, a subject of which his fellow guests then knew nothing. The next morning Haddon sailed for Liverpool, and Mrs. Jayne, with characteristic American energy, went to St. Louis, found the Red Indians in question, and from them learnt, among other things, how to make the Tent Flap. That was the beginning of her interest in the subject, which in its early days owed much to her enterprise.

It is made thus :—*First*, Opening A. *Second*, Lift the loops off the index-fingers, pass them over their corresponding hands on to the wrists, thus making them dorsal strings. *Third*, Bend each thumb away from you over one string, and with its back pick up from below the next string, and return. *Fourth*, Bend each little-finger towards you, and with its back pick up the next string. *Fifth*, Grasp with the left hand all the strings in the centre of the figure where they cross, pass this bunch of strings from the palmar side between the right thumb and index-finger so that the bunch lies along the arm, with the left thumb and index-finger take hold of the two loops on the right thumb, draw them over the tip of the right thumb, let the bunch of strings also slip over the right thumb to the palmar side, and then replace the two loops on the right thumb ; make a similar movement with the other hand. *Lastly*, Lift the wrist loops over the hands, letting them fall on the front or palmar sides of the hands, rub the hands together, separate them, and the figure will appear.

The working may be summarized thus :—Opening A. Index strings over the hands on to the wrists. Each thumb over one and picks up one. Each little-finger picks up one. Thumb loops over groups of strings. Wrist loops over hands. Extend.

8. *CROW'S FEET* (Class A) ; for diagram, see page 19, figure 6. This figure, also, is mentioned and delineated in my Lecture, and I have nothing more to say about it. It is the most generally spread of string patterns at present known, occurring in Africa, Australasia, the Pacific Isles, America, and sporadically elsewhere. It may be native to

Great Britain, where it is called the *Leashing of Lochiel's Dogs*, but it seems more likely that it was introduced here by sailors. It has many alternative names.

It is made thus :—*First*, Opening A. *Second*, Insert the four fingers of each hand from above into the corresponding thumb loops, and throw the near thumb string over the closed thumbs and fingers on to the backs of the hands. *Third*, Transfer each index-finger loop to the corresponding thumb. *Fourth*, Transfer each dorsal loop to one of the free digits of that hand, for choice I prefer the index-finger. *Fifth*, Pass each near little-finger string from below through the corresponding index-finger loop, place it on the far side of the little-finger, and Navaho the far little-finger strings. *Lastly*, Release the thumbs and extend. In the working of this figure in different places there are many small variations.

If the middle strings of the final figure are held by the teeth, the hands placed horizontally with their palms upmost, and the strings stretched, the result closely resembles the figure of *Two Hogans*, as made in Arizona, representing the poles of two small tents side by side.

9. *LIGHTNING* (Class A): for diagram, see page 3, figure 1. In my Lecture I described and showed this figure, and gave its construction; I need not here repeat this. It was obtained from Red Indians who live on the border of Arizona, where ethnologists have been fortunate in finding natives able to describe old tribal customs and amusements; it has also been found in New Caledonia. It is an excellent example, but the last movement may present difficulty to a beginner.

The working may be summarized thus :—The Navaho

Opening. Each thumb over two and picks up one. Each mid-finger over one and picks up one. Each ring-finger over one, and picks up one. Each little-finger over one, and picks up one. Release thumbs, put them into the spaces by the little-fingers, and rest them on the near little-finger string. Throw the loose hanging strings to the back of the figure, press down the thumbs, and turn the hands to face away from you.

10. *LITTLE FISHES* (Class A). This figure was obtained in the Torres Straits; the final pattern somewhat resembles Lightning. The first movement in the construction is unusual.

It is made thus :—*First*, Insert the index-fingers, pointing upwards, into the loop of string so that the far index string

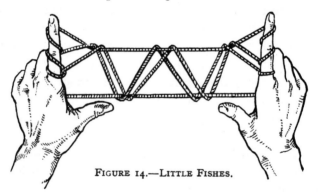

FIGURE 14.—LITTLE FISHES.

is short and straight; next, take hold of each side of this far index string between the tips of the corresponding thumb and index-finger and form with it a small upright ring, say, by carrying the part of string held by the left hand towards you and to the right over the right hand string; put the index-fingers away from you into this ring, and separate the hands;

this is called the *Murray Opening*. *Second*, Bend each thumb over the lower near index string, and with its back pick up, from below, the lower far index string; then bend each thumb over the upper near index string, and with its back pick up, from below, the upper far index string; next, bend each little-finger over the upper near index string, and with its back pick up, from below, the lower near index string. Extend. *Lastly*, Pass the tip of each index-finger away from you and close to the base of the little-finger into the triangle resting on that finger, and bending the index-finger towards you and then upwards, pick up with its back the upper near index string; turn the palms from you, thus releasing the thumbs, and extend.

The natives make the figure to a sing-song chant, " Little fishes swim round to Waier Waier in the channel, to Waier Waier in the channel," and so on.

The working may be summarised thus :—Murray Opening. Each thumb over one string of the lower loop, picks up the next, then over one string of the upper loop, and picks up the next. Each little-finger over one and picks up one. Each index-finger from above into far triangle, and picks up on its back the upper near index string. Rotate, release thumbs, and extend.

11. *THE VEILED SUN* or *AN ECLIPSE* (Class A). This is a widely distributed figure known in the Torres Straits as the *Mouth*, and in Queensland as the *Veiled Sun*. It also occurs in the Andaman Isles, in the Caroline Isles as one stage in a figure known as *Carrying Stone-Money*, and in Central Africa as one stage in a figure known as the *Eclipsed Moon*. In native practice, these continuations involve taking the design completely off the hands, placing it on the knees, and

re-arranging the strings ; in my opinion such constructions are not to be commended.

The Eclipse is made thus :—*First*, Opening A. *Second*, Take the far little-finger string in the mouth, bring it over the other loops, and release the little-fingers. *Third*, Pass each little-finger over both strings of the index loop, and on its back

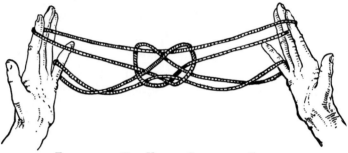

FIGURE 15.—THE VEILED SUN OR AN ECLIPSE.

pick up the far thumb string ; return, and release the thumbs. *Fourth*, Insert each index-finger, from below and close to the mouth into the mouth loop, release the mouth, and extend. *Lastly*, Navaho the index loops. In making this figure the strings should be kept rather loose. The working affords a good example of the way in which the mouth may be used to facilitate a construction.

12. *A FISHING NET* (Class A) ; for diagram, see page 19, figure 7. This figure is mentioned and delineated in my Lecture. It has been found in Africa, Oregon, and the Hawaiian Isles. In some places it is called *Quadruple Diamonds*, in others a *Ladder*, and in others a *Fence*.

It is made thus :—*First*, Opening A. *Second*, Release the thumbs, then bend them away from you under four strings, and with their backs pick up the far little-finger string, and return. *Third*, Bend each thumb away from you over one string, and with its back pick up the next string. *Fourth*, Release the little-fingers, then bend each of them towards you over one string, and with its back pick up the next string. *Fifth*, Release the thumbs, then bend each of them away from you over two strings, and with its back pick up the next string. *Sixth*, Pick up from the base of each index-finger the near index string, and put it over the corresponding thumb, and Navaho the thumb loops. *Seventh*, Put each index-finger from above into the adjacent triangle, whose sides are formed by the radial little-finger string twisting round the two strings of the thumb loop. *Lastly*, Rotate the hands so as to face away from you (thus causing the little-finger loops and the lower index loops to fall off, the thumbs to point away from you, and the index-fingers to point upwards), and separate the hands.

The working may be summarized thus :—Opening A. Release thumbs. Each thumb under all the strings, and picks up the far string. Each thumb over one, and picks up one. Release little-fingers. Each little-finger over one, and picks up one. Release thumbs. Each thumb over two and picks up one. Each near index string on tip of corresponding thumb. Navaho the loops on the thumbs. Index-fingers in triangles. Rotate the hands, releasing little-fingers, and extend.

13. *A BUTTERFLY* (Class A). This, like Lightning, is a Navaho figure ; it was first obtained by Jayne in 1904. It represents the insect with its wings up. The working is more simple than the description suggests.

The figure is made thus :—*First*, Take up the string in the

Navaho way, that is make the first movement as when forming Lightning. *Second,* Twist each index loop by rotating the index-finger down toward you and up again four or five times. *Third,* Bend each thumb away from you over one string, with its back pick up the next string, and Navaho the thumb loops. *Fourth,* Put the tip of the index-finger of one hand against the

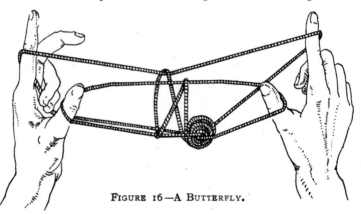

FIGURE 16—A BUTTERFLY.

tip of the index-finger of the other hand and similarly put the tips of the thumbs together; then slip the right index loop on to the tip of the left index-finger and the right thumb loop on to the tip of the left thumb, thus freeing the right hand. *Fifth,* Put the tips of the right index-finger and thumb against the left thumb between the two strings on that hand, then slip the right index-finger away from you under the loop on the tip of the left thumb, and slip the right thumb towards you under the loop at the base of the left thumb. *Sixth,* With the right thumb and index-finger lift both loops from the left index-finger; then put the left index-finger away from you into the loop previously on the tip of that finger, and the left thumb towards you into the loop previously at the base of that finger. *Lastly*, Draw the hands apart and when the strings have partially rolled up in the middle of the figure, use the free fingers of each hand to pull down the far index string and the near thumb string. The butterfly will now appear ; its wings being held up by the string extended between the widely separated thumbs and index-fingers.

The working may be summarized thus :—Navaho Opening. Twist index loops. Each thumb over one and picks up one. Navaho the thumb loops. Take up figure afresh with thumbs and index-fingers, and extend.

14. *THE LAIA FRUIT* (Class A). This was found by T. T. Barnard in the New Hebrides in 1923. The result is a pyramid with an hexagonal base; it is an effective design and easy to make, but being in three dimensions does not lend itself well to illustration by a diagram.

It is made thus:—*First*, Opening A. *Second*, Insert the four fingers of each hand from above into the corresponding thumb loops, throw the near thumb string over the closed thumbs and fingers on to the backs of the hands, and put the thumbs into the wrist loop. *Third*, Turn the right thumb down under both the wrist strings, pass it from below into the little finger loop, with its back pick up the far little finger string, and return. *Fourth*, Insert the left thumb, from the near side and from below, into the right thumb loop (close to the thumb), and extend. *Fifth*, Transfer the index loops to the little-fingers. *Sixth*, With each little-finger take up the corresponding far thumb string. *Seventh*, With each index-finger take up from below both the near little finger strings, and release the thumbs. *Lastly*, With the back of each thumb take up from below that near index string which is a continuation of the near wrist string, release the little fingers, and extend.

The same figure though differently placed on the hands can be made by interchanging all the movements from back to front and vice versa: for instance, using the little-fingers instead of the thumbs, substituting far for near, and so on: in this form it is known as the *Laia Flower*.

15. *CAT'S CRADLE* (Class A). The various forms of this figure are made successively by two persons, P and Q, each of whom in turn takes the string off the hands of the other, and draws his hands apart so as to stretch the string. I have dealt with its history in my Lecture.

In the following description the terms *near* and *far* refer to the player from whom the string is being taken. In the nursery form of this game there are four standard forms, delineated below. Normally these are made as follows :—

The weaving begins by P twisting the string round the four fingers of each hand so as to make two dorsal strings and one palmar string, next picking up the string on the palm of each hand with the back of the mid-finger of the other hand, and then drawing the hands apart ; this forms the *Cradle*. The figure comprises two horizontal strings, over each of which are crossed strings, each cross has four angles, which we may describe, with reference to P, as the right and left, upper and lower.

In the second stage, Q (facing P) inserts, from the side of the figure nearest P, his right thumb in to the left angle of the near cross and his right index-finger into the right angle of this cross ; and from the side of the figure farthest from P, his left

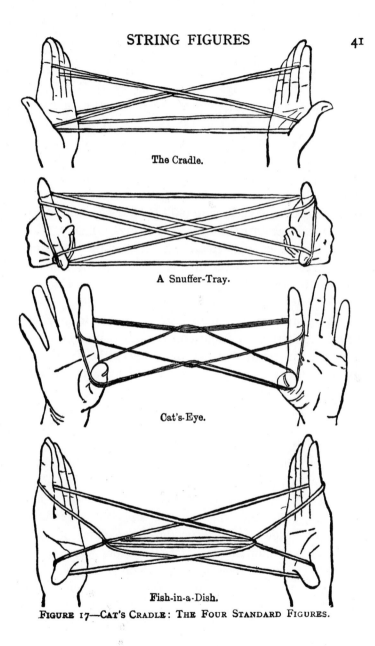

The Cradle.

A Snuffer-Tray.

Cat's-Eye.

Fish-in-a-Dish.

FIGURE 17—CAT'S CRADLE: THE FOUR STANDARD FIGURES.

thumb into the left angle of the far cross, and his left index-finger into the right angle of this cross. Next, Q with the tips of the thumbs and index-fingers, takes hold of each cross pulls it away from the centre of the figure, over and beyond the corresponding horizontal string, and continuing the motion carries the cross round this string ; Q then turns his thumbs and fingers upwards through a right angle, thus passing the cross between the two horizontal strings, which causes the thumbs and index-finger of each hand (still holding the crossed strings) to be brought against the horizontal strings. Lastly, Q having pushed his fingers up, releases the crosses by separating his index-fingers from his thumbs, and drawing his hands apart removes the string from P's hand. This pattern is called a *Snuffer-Tray* ; the diagram on page 41 represents it as seen by P. The figure lies in a horizontal plane, and comprises two two straight strings and four crosses. Of these crosses we are only concerned with those at the sides of the figure, and in each of them the angles may be described, with reference to Q, as right and left, near and far.

In the third stage, P (facing Q) inserts, from below, his left thumb into the left angle of the side cross farthest from Q, and his left index-finger into the right angle of this cross, his right thumb into the left angle of the side cross nearest Q and his right index-finger into the right angle of this cross. Next, P with the tips of his thumbs and index-fingers, takes hold of each cross, pulls it down, separates his hands, thus bringing each cross below its corresponding horizontal string, and continuing the motion carries the cross outside, round, and above this string. P then turns each thumb and finger towards the centre of the figure between the two horizontal strings, through two right angles, taking these strings with them. Lastly P pushes his fingers down, separates the index-fingers from the thumbs, and then drawing his hands apart, removes the figure from Q's hand. The resulting figure is known as *Cat's Eye* ; the diagram on page 41 shows it as seen by Q, after the figure has been made. It lies in a horizontal plane with P's fingers pointing downwards and comprises four crosses ; of these crosses we are only concerned with those at the sides of the figure, and in each of them the angles may be described with reference to P as right and left, near and far.

In the final stage, Q, inserts, from above, his left thumb into the left angle of the cross farthest P, his left index-finger into the right angle of this cross, and his right thumb into the left angle of the cross nearest P, and his right index-finger into the right angle of this cross. Next, Q turns each hand inwards towards the centre of the figure, through two right angles, and as he does so catches the sides of the centre diamond on the thumb and index-fingers ; and the end of this motion the thumbs and fingers will be pointing upwards. Lastly, Q draws his hands apart, and thus takes the figure off P's hands. The diagram on page 41 represents the pattern as seen by Q. This forms *Fish-in-a-dish*, the fish being represented by the two parallel lines in the middle of the design, and the dish by the diamond-shaped figure on which they rest.

16. *OTHER FIGURES IN CLASS A.* Numerous other easy and attractive figures in class A will be found in Jayne accompanied by full workings and much historical information ; as good examples I pick out *Double Diamonds*, a simplified form of the Fishing Net described above, the net having two meshes instead of four, found among the Oklahoma Indians

and in Hawaii ; *Two Chiefs* or *Two Caterpillars* side by side, from Uap in the Caroline Isles ; and the *Square*, a modern invention. An instructive group of figures is afforded by *Meshed Networks* ; one form of such a pattern, as made in West Africa, is called a *Face Mark*, and another very similar figure, as made by Red Indians, is known as *Many Stars* ; of these the general design is obtained most simply by the negro method, but the American working may be easily altered so as to give slight variations in the final pattern, thus introducing the operator to the amusement of making new figures. Another good design is *Circles and Triangles*, from the Natiks in the Caroline Isles, in which a series of loops are gracefully intertwined.

Of effective but harder examples, here commended by me with more hesitation, I may mention a *Rabbit*, from Red Indians in Oregon ; a *Sea-Gull* from the Eskimo ; *Two Elks* from the Klamath Indians ; and *Tree Burial*, from Papua.

References for the workings of these additional figures are given below under the heading, " Authorities."

CLASS B. Of figures in class B, I select the following as being easy and interesting: —the *Mosquito* or *Fly*, a *Siberian House*, the *Elusive Loop*, *Fluttering Wings*, the *Yam Thief* or *Uprooting the Alou*, *Throwing a Spear*, a *Man Climbing a Tree*, the *Sleeper*, a *Well*, a *Fence*, a *Salmon-Net*, the *Caterpillar*, the *Ebbing Tide*, and the *Porker*.

17. *THE MOSQUITO OR FLY* (Class B). This is one of the easiest of the β constructions. I worked it in my Lecture in its South American form. Figures resembling it, and somewhat similarly made, have been found in many places, but the variety here given is the simplest of them. The result shows the

insect with its body midway between the hands and its wings spread out.

It is made thus :—*First*, Put the thumbs, held upright, into the loop of string, and extend. *Second*, Move the left hand to face away from you; then turn it counter-clockwise under the strings and up towards you into its normal position, thus giving two dorsal strings, and no palmar string. *Third*, Pass

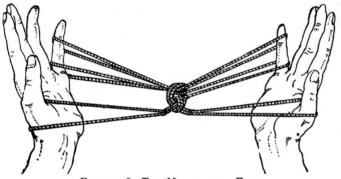

FIGURE 18—THE MOSQUITO OR FLY.

the right hand between you and the left hand, then put the right little-finger from above under the dorsal strings, pick them up, and return. *Fourth*, Put the left little-finger on the right palm, and pass it towards you under the two strings on the right thumb, pick them up, and return. *Lastly*, Lift the dorsal strings on the left hand over the digits, and extend. This is the Mosquito or Fly.

Next its proboscis (or some part of its anatomy) is shown by releasing the little-fingers. To try to catch the insect, clap your hands together: on drawing them apart quickly and as far as possible, it will always be found that it has escaped, in fact the display of the proboscis destroyed the figure.

Ethnologists, more conservative than primitive men, deem it undesirable or worse to vary recorded methods, so with hesitation I add that the Indians might have made the conclusion more effective by not displaying the proboscis and thus not destroying the mosquito as a definite creation; in this case, as before, on trying to squash it, you clap your hands sharply together, then drawing them apart quickly and at the same time releasing the little-fingers, it will have disappeared. Of course with a mosquito or fly between one's hands the most natural thing is to try to squash it, but often, as here represented, without success.

The knot in the figure midway between the hands may also be taken to represent a coco-nut, and Compton reports that in Lifu, in a similar figure, the last movement is used to illustrate efforts to crush the shell. The unskilful person, when clapping his hands and not releasing his little-fingers, fails, for on separating his hands the nut remains visible. But when the skilled native tries, then on clapping his hands and simultaneously releasing his little-fingers, he succeeds, for on separating his hands the nut is broken and gone.

18. *A SIBERIAN HOUSE* (Class B). This was obtained from the Eskimo, who are experts in making string figures.

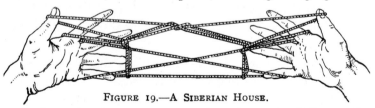

FIGURE 19.—A SIBERIAN HOUSE.

It is made thus :—*First*, Opening A. *Second*, Insert the four fingers of each hand from above into the corresponding

thumb loops, and throw the near thumb string over the closed
thumbs and fingers on to the backs of the hands. *Third*, Bend
each thumb from you over one string, under all the others,
and with its back pick up the far string which comes round
from the back of the hand. *Lastly*, Pull the dorsal string,
which lies on the back of each hand, over the fingers on to the
front of that hand, and extend. This is the House.

There are two boys inside the house. If you do not see
them, release the index fingers, and draw the hands apart.
The house will then break up, and the boys will be seen escaping,
one from each side.

19. *THE ELUSIVE LOOP* (Class B). This consists in
making a loop, representing (say) a yam, to be offered to a
hungry applicant. The operator causes the yam to disappear
unless it is seized sufficiently promptly ; hence a contest in
rapidity between the operator and the applicant. Alternatively
you can display the yam, and when the applicant asks for food
make it disappear, remarking that you have none, or if you prefer,
none for him. There are figures of this type common in all
countries, and any of them will answer the purpose of the game.

A simple construction, common in Great Britain (and
best illustrated with a loop of string some two to two-and-
a-half feet long) is as follows :—*First*, Put the four fingers of
the left hand, held vertically with its palm facing you, into
the loop, giving a short straight piece of string across the
palm of the hand and a loose loop at its back, and hook, from
below, into this dorsal loop the right index-finger. *Second*, Bring
the right index-finger vertically over the left hand so as to
make that string of the dorsal loop which is next the left
index-finger pass between the left index and middle fingers

and that string of the loop which is next the left little-finger pass between the left little and ring fingers, thus forming one loop on the left index-finger and another on the left little-finger. *Third*, Move the right index-finger so as to bring the two strings hooked on it (keeping the ulnar above the radial string) between the left index-finger and thumb, and then round the thumb ; next pass the left little-finger, from below, between these strings (the former radial string being ulnar to it), and then carry the right index-finger to the right in front of the left hand. *Fourth*, Turn the right index-finger clockwise through two right angles, thus putting a twist on the loop held by it, and then transfer this loop to the left index-finger, releasing the right index-finger. *Lastly*, with the right thumb and index-finger lift the two loops off the left thumb and put them, from the front, between the left middle and ring fingers. The loop thus placed on the back of the left hand is the Elusive Loop. On pulling the left palmar string this loop will disappear, and the string come free off the hand

20. *FLUTTERING WINGS* (Class B). This comes from Murray Island, where the movements are described as those of a tern.

It is made thus:—*First*, Opening A. *Second*, Put the foot (or a heavy book) over the far string so as to hold it down. *Third*, With the back of each little-finger pick up, from below, the far index-finger string; and Navaho the little-finger loops. *Fourth*, With the back of each thumb pick up, from below, the near index-finger string; and Navaho the thumb loops. *Lastly*, Release the index-fingers.

In the resulting figure the long loop on the foot (or book) is supposed to represent the extended neck and body of the bird,

and the index and thumb loops its wings.   By rotating the
wrists the wings flutter.

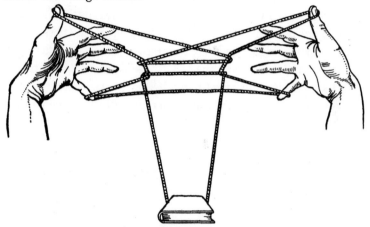

FIGURE 20.—FLUTTERING WINGS.

21. *THE YAM THIEF* (Class B).   This is a good illustration of a string story ; one version of it is given in my Lecture,
and a drawing of the final arrangement also appears there,
see page 7, figure 4.   Among some tribes the result is said
to represent the flight of a row of birds sitting on a rail and
suddenly disturbed; among others it is used to illustrate a
story about a cat and a mouse.   In Lifu it is called *Uprooting*
the Alou; the strings on the hand representing the root; and
the palmar string a shoot of that tree.   Someone, representing
a strong stupid man, takes hold of the shoot, and though he
pulls for all he is worth and is encouraged by the shouts of the
onlookers, he cannot move the root: then someone else, representing the traditional cunning village clown, takes hold
of the shoot and (the thumb loop being released) the root comes
up easily, to the ostensible astonishment of the spectators.   This

design is widely distributed, and has been found in Africa,
America, Oceania, Siberia, and Japan.

The figure is made thus :—*First*, Hold the left hand open
with the palm facing you, the thumb upright and the fingers
pointing to the right and slightly upwards. With the right
hand, loop the string over the left thumb, crossing the strings
if you like, and let one string hang down over the palm and the
other over the back of the hand—we may call these the palmar
and the dorsal strings. *Second*, Pass the right index-finger
from below under the palmar string, and then between the left
thumb and index-finger, and with its front tip hook up a loop
of the dorsal string; pull this loop between the left thumb
and index-finger back on to the left palm; then with the right
index-finger give the loop one twist clockwise, and put it over
the palmar string on to the left index-finger; pull the two
pendant strings so as to tighten the loops on the thumb and
index-finger. *Third*, In the same way pass the right index-
finger from below under the pendant palmar string, and then
between the left index and middle fingers, and with its front
tip hook up another piece of the pendant dorsal string; pull
this loop back on to the left palm, and with the right index-
finger give the loop one twist clockwise, and put it over the
palmar string on the left mid-finger. *Fourth*, In the same
way, working between the middle and ring fingers, hook up
another loop of the pendant dorsal string, and put it on the left
ring-finger. *Fifth*, In the same way, working between the ring
and little-fingers, pick up another loop of the pendant dorsal
string, and put it on left little-finger. *Sixth*, Take off the left
thumb loop, and hold it between the left thumb and index-
finger ; and, for the sake of effect, to show that the loops are

still on the fingers, pull the pendant dorsal string. *Lastly,* Pull the pendant palmar string, and the figure will come off the hand.

22. *THROWING A SPEAR* (Class B). This is a rather dull figure, but is easy to construct; it has been found in Queensland, Africa, and the Torres Straits. In some places it is known as a *Canoe.*

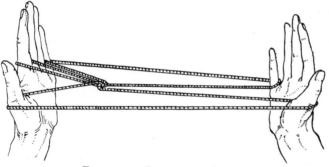

FIGURE 21—THROWING A SPEAR.

It is made thus :—*First,* Opening A. *Second,* Transfer the right index loop to the tip of the left index, and pass the original left index string over this on to the right index. *Lastly,* Release the right index and extend, bringing the right thumb and little-finger close together. We thus get a spear with a heavy handle on the right hand, and three prongs resting on the left hand.

To throw the spear from one hand to the other pass the right index from below under the string just dropped from the right index, up to the left index, and with its back pick up this string. Release the left index, and the spear flies to the other hand. This can be repeated over and over again.

23. *A MAN CLIMBING A TREE* (Class B); for diagram, see page 6, figure 3. This is a figure derived from the Blacks in Queensland, and is one of the most effective examples of class B. It is described and delineated in my Lecture. It is suggested that the two upright strings represent the trunk of a tree and the loops which move up these strings represent the arms and feet (or tree band and feet) of a man climbing up it.

It is made thus :—*First*, Opening A. *Second*, Bend each little-finger towards you over four strings, with its back pick up the next string, and return. *Third*, Navaho the little-finger loops. *Fourth*, Bend each index-finger over the palmar string and between the two strings of the loop on that finger and press its tip on the palm. *Fifth*, Holding the strings loosely, slip the loops off the thumbs; then still keeping the tips of the index-fingers on the palms, separate the hands, thus causing the loops near the bases of those fingers to slip over the knuckles and so off the fingers. *Lastly*, Put the far little finger string under one foot, or under a heavy book, release the little-fingers, and pull gently with the index-fingers, after hooking their tips into the string they hold. This makes the "man" climb up the "tree."

24. *THE SLEEPER* (Class B). This is a Torres Straits figure, in my opinion dull in itself and not suggestive of the supposed object, but experience shows, pleasing to some people.

It is made thus :—*First*, Opening A. *Second*, Pass each thumb from you over the far thumb string and under both strings of the index loop ; pick up on its back the near little-finger string, and return the thumb under the index loop.

Third, Pass each little-finger towards you over the far index string, under the near index string, pick up on its back the far thumb string (not the palmar string), and return the little-

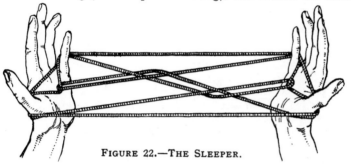

FIGURE 22.—THE SLEEPER.

finger under the near index string. *Lastly*, Release the index-fingers, and extend.

This gives a figure supposed to represent a bed or hammock with a man lying on it. Having reached this stage the natives sing " Man on a bed, man on a bed, lies asleep, lies asleep, bed breaks," and on the word " breaks " they release the little-fingers with unpleasant results to the suppositious sleeper.

25. *A WELL* (Class B). This figure has been found in Lifu, Murray Isle, and Mabuiag. It is also known as a *Canoe* and as a *Nest*.

It is made thus :—*First*, Opening A. *Second*, Insert each index-finger from above, into the little-finger loop ; bend the finger down over the far index and near little-finger strings ; then, hooking these strings on it, pass it between the far thumb and near index strings, and let the index loops slip off. Release the little-fingers. *Third*, Insert each little-finger, from above, into the index loops, and with it pull down the two far index strings, bringing the hands into their normal position.

Fourth, Give a twist to each thumb loop by taking hold of the far thumb string, pulling the loop off the thumb, and then replacing the loop on the thumb with this string on the near side of the thumb. *Lastly,* With the back of each thumb pick up the lower part of the string passing obliquely from the near

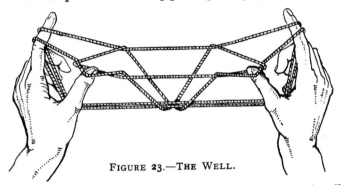

FIGURE 23.—THE WELL.

side of the index-finger to the two bottom strings, and pull it through the thumb loop, thus allowing that loop to slip off.

The inverted pyramid in the centre of the figure represents the Well. The Well can be filled by slacking the little-fingers, and pulling the thumb and index strings; this movement raises the bottom of the Well.

The working may be summarized thus :—Opening A. Each index hooks far index and little-finger strings, and carries them between the thumb and index strings. Little-fingers pull down the far index strings. Twist to thumb loops. Each thumb picks up the oblique string, and pulls it through the thumb loop.

26. *A FENCE* (Class B). In the Loyalty Isles the natives continue the construction to make a figure known as a Fence Round the Well. This is really a figure in class A, but since

it is a continuation of one in class B it is, perhaps somewhat illogically, treated as being in the latter class.

It is made thus :—*First*, Make the Well. *Second*, Bend each thumb away from you close to the index-finger under the two near index strings, and with its back pick up these two strings. *Third*, Navaho the lowest string on each thumb, that

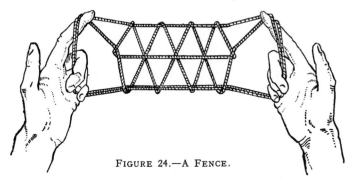

FIGURE 24.—A FENCE.

is, lift it over the two strings on the tip of the thumb, and drop it on the palmar side of the hand. *Fourth*, Release gently the little and index-fingers, thus allowing the figure to hang loosely on the thumbs. *Lastly*, Put the four fingers of each hand towards you into the thumb loops close to the thumbs ; press the middle, ring, and little fingers on the palm ; release the thumbs, raise the index-fingers, and extend.

The working may be summarized thus :—Make the Well. Each thumb picks up the two near index strings, and returns through the thumb loops. Release all fingers. All fingers of each hand through the thumb loops ; release thumbs ; raise the index fingers.

A similar figure made by the Yöruba negroes in West Africa is taken to show a corpse (represented by the straight cross string) being taken in a canoe or sledge (represented by the network) for burial.

27. *A SALMON NET* (Class B). A *Salmon Net*, or *Triple Diamonds*, or *Caroline Diamonds* is a net-work of three meshes placed side by side ; it may be of negro origin, but comes to us from the Natiks in the Caroline Isles.

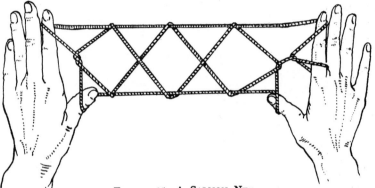

FIGURE 25—A SALMON NET.

It is made thus :—*First*, Opening A. *Second*, Take the right hand out of the string, and put the tips of the right thumb and little-finger together from the right side into the left index loop, extend, and release the left index. *Third*, With the back of the right index-finger pick up the string on the palm of the left hand. *Fourth*, Bend each thumb from you over one string, and with its back pick up the next string, keeping it on the tip of the thumb. *Fifth*, Bend each index-finger towards you, and with the extreme tip of its back pick up the next string. *Sixth*, Navaho the thumb loops. *Lastly*, Release the little-fingers, rotating the hands so as to face away from you, and extend ; beginners sometimes find this last movement difficult.

At the end, an onlooker puts his hand, representing a salmon, in the middle mesh. It escapes if the left hand is released and the right hand moved away, but is caught if the right hand is released and the left hand moved away.

28. *THE CATERPILLAR* (Class B). This design is known in North Australia, and various places in Southern Oceania ; it is described by Jayne under the name *One Chief*.

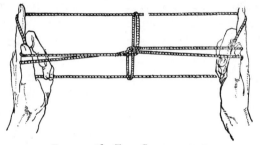

FIGURE 26—THE CATERPILLAR.

The result shows the outline of what may be taken to be a caterpillar, which can be made to loop itself up, and so crawl forwards.

The Caterpillar is made thus :—*First*, Take up the string in the form of the First Position (see p. 20), and then put a loop round the left thumb. *Second*, With the back of the right index pick up the left thumb loop ; pass the left index through the right index loop and, with its back, pick up the right palmar string ; pass the right index through the left index loop, and with its back, pick up the left palmar string. *Third*, Release the left hand ; hold the right hand horizontal and palm downwards, and put the loop which is nearer the tip of the right index over the loop which is nearer the base of that finger. *Fourth*, Put the left little-finger and thumb towards you between the two

loops on the right index and resting on the joint of the finger ;
and, with the back of the left little-finger, pick up the adjacent
loop now nearer the base of the right index, and with the back
of the left thumb, pick up the adjacent loop now nearer the tip
of the right index ; extend, thus pulling both loops off the
right index. *Fifth*, Transfer each thumb loop to the corresponding index-finger, and then transfer it back again by
putting the thumb from outside into the loop. (The
effect of this is to turn the thumb loops over.) *Sixth*, Bend each
thumb from you over one string, and, with its back, pick up
the next string. *Seventh*, Put each index-finger over the palmar
string under the far thumb string, and, with its back, pick
up on the far tip of the finger the latter string, hold it
against the index-finger by the mid-finger, erect the index
fingers, thus bringing the string connecting their tips to
the top of the figure, and rotate the wrists away from you.
Lastly. Keeping the thumbs and index-fingers close together,
bend down the little and ring fingers, and, with their tips,
catch and stretch the far string, thus making sure that it is
brought to the bottom of the figure.   Extend flat on the knee,
and the caterpillar appears.

If the wrists are now turned so as to move the palms of
the hands upwards, the caterpillar will contract.   Then turn
them back to their former position, and he elongates. Repeat
the action, and he walks down the leg.

29.   *THE EBBING TIDE* (Class B).   This was obtained
from Lifu where it is known as *Sardines*.   It has also been
found in Queensland under the name *Shrimps*, in Papua under
the name of the *Coral Reef*, and in Mebu where it is used to
illustrate the passing of men along a road.   It and the next

figure are not difficult, but take somewhat longer to make than those I have previously described : that is a defect. They are, however, so excellent of their kind that I put them among my selected examples, and commend them to my readers.

The construction involves an initial movement followed by the Lifu movement, each comprising four steps.

Initial Movement : (i.) Navaho Opening, as in Lightning. (ii.) Pass each little-finger over one string and with its back pick up, from below, the near index string; release the index-fingers. (iii.) Bend each thumb over one string, and with its back pick up, from below, the near little-finger string. (iv.) With the back of the tip of each index-finger pick up, from below, the far thumb string, with the thumb press the part of this string now on the near side of the index-finger against it, and turn the palms away from you. This step is known as the " Caroline Extension." At the end of this movement we get two widely separated parallel strings, one at the top and the other at the bottom of the figure, and in front of them across the middle of the figure two strings close together. The figure represents high tide.

The Lifu Movement : (i.) Release the thumbs ; pass each thumb under the index and little-finger loops, and, then from below, into the index loop. (ii.) Rotate each thumb away from you downwards, and then up, thus picking up on its back the far index string, and putting a twist on each thumb loop; release the index-fingers. (iii.) With the back of each thumb pick up, from below, the near little-finger string. (iv.) Make the Caroline Extension. At the end of this movement, we get two diamonds representing two rocks which appear as the tide ebbs.

Repeating the Lifu Movement we get four rocks, and every further repetition of it shows two more rocks. In Mebu, the successive results are said to represent an empty path, two men walking along it, then four men, and so on. In Kiwi, the same story is told about women.

The Flowing Tide. In my Lecture a continuation of the figure was shown by Mrs. Rishbeth, by which it was transformed, so that each further repetition of the Lifu Movement caused two rocks to disappear, and finally there was again high tide. To effect this we interpolate at the end of one of the Lifu Movements the following *Reversing Movement*, with the object of turning the whole figure counter-clockwise through two right angles. (i.) Release the index-fingers and extend, spreading out the fingers. (ii.) Take the two near left thumb strings in the mouth (or preferably, if wearing the usual garments of civilized man, hang these strings on the top button of the jacket or waistcoat), and release the left hand. (iii.) Put the left thumb and little-finger, tip to tip, against those of the right hand, and slip the loops from the right hand on to the corresponding digits of the left hand. (iv.) With the left thumb and index-finger, take hold from the right of the two strings on the right side of the button and close to it, and lift them off the button, allowing them to hang vertically as parts of two loops: then, turning these strings round counter-clockwise through two right angles, put the right little-finger away from you into the pendant loop originally on the left little-finger, and the right thumb away from you into both these pendant loops; release the two strings held by the left hand and taken off the button; bring the hands into their normal position, and extend. This fourth step requires care ; if correctly performed, the same string is now ulnar to (i.e. the far string of) both the little-fingers, and the figure is symmetrically placed on the two hands, there being two radial strings on each thumb. (v.) Make the Caroline Extension, and you get a figure resembling that from which you started at the beginning of the Reversing Movement. Every successive Lifu Movement will now cause two rocks to disappear, until finally we come again to high tide.

This is an excellent example of a String Figure ; the working showing successively high tide, the gradual ebb, dead low water, and then the reverse flow, until we again get high tide. If you then continue to make the Lifu Movement the tide will again ebb.

30. *THE PORKER* (Class B). This figure was obtained from Lifu by R. H. Compton; it is also known in Uvea. The result is particularly effective.

It is made thus :—*First*, Make Little Fishes (see page 34), giving a W-shaped pattern. *Second*, With the back of each thumb take up the corresponding outer arm of the W ; release from each index-finger the three loops on it, and extend. *Third*, Pass each index-finger, from below, into the corresponding thumb loop, and on its back take up the far thumb string, letting its continuation slip off the thumb. *Fourth*, Pass the thumbs under the index loops (thus releasing the thumb loops), over the far little-finger string, then with its back pick up the latter string and return below the whole figure. You now have a loop on each thumb, index, and little finger, the near string of each thumb loop passing below the far string of that loop, crossing the palm below the index loop, passing below the near string of the little-finger loop, and becoming the far string of the little-finger loop. The resulting figure is said to represent the outline of a long low island near Lifu, having three headlands at each end.

Fifth, We have next to put the thumb and little-finger loops on each hand above the strings of the index loop. To effect this, we pass the right thumb and index-finger, from above, through the left index loop ; lift the left thumb loop off that digit, bring it up through the left index loop, and replace it unaltered on the left thumb ; do the same with the left little-finger loop. Make corresponding movements with the other hand. *Sixth*, Take each index loop, and put it over the whole hand on to the back of the wrist. [Thus placed, these strings serve to make the legs of the porker.] With the right thumb and index-finger, take hold of the far left thumb and near left little-finger strings, and remove the left hand. With the left thumb and index-finger take hold of these two strings where they are held by the right thumb and index-finger, releasing them from the right hand. With the left thumb and index-finger take hold also of the two corresponding right-hand strings, and remove the right hand. The left thumb and index-finger now grasp four loops, namely, the two original thumb loops and the two original little-finger loops.

Seventh, Pass the right thumb and little-finger towards the left hand and between the two original thumb loops, and separating these digits take up on their backs these two loops. With the right thumb and index-finger take hold of the two other loops held by the left thumb and index-finger, and release the left hand. Pass the left thumb and little-finger between the two original little-finger loops, and separating these digits take up on their backs these two loops. Extend. *Lastly*,

With the tips of the index and middle fingers of the right hand hold and slightly raise the two middle strings going to that hand; release the right thumb and little-finger; then pass the middle, ring, and little-fingers of the right hand below and round the two strings going to the right hand, and let the index-finger follow them. These two strings are now hooked on and held by the four fingers of the right hand. You now

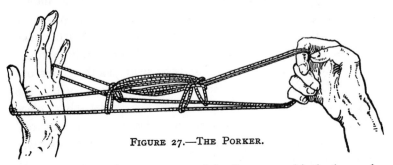

FIGURE 27.—THE PORKER.

have a quadruped as represented in figure 27, his body made of eight strings and each leg of two strings. By gently pulling the two upper strings on the right hand the porker walks towards the right, by pulling the two lower strings, he walks to the left. During his progress you can address him in whatever terms you deem suitable. The final figure is slightly improved if, at the end of the last movement, we raise, with the tip of the mid-finger of the left hand, the two middle strings going to that hand, and hold them in place by pressing the index finger against them. This step, however, is not essential to the working, and is not given by Compton.

31. *OTHER FIGURES IN CLASS B.* Other excellent examples in class B are the following:—*Two Lads,* from New

Caledonia; in this the two lads run out of shelter, and then when frightened run back again, and continue such advances and retreats as often as is wished. *Two Eyes*, if I may give them that name, from the Yöruba Negroes in West Africa; in this the eyes alternately open and close. *Two Boys Fighting for an Arrow*, from Red Indians in Oregon: in this two loops representing the boys are held by the index-fingers; if a twig be put into the middle of the completed figure, the index-fingers released, and the figure extended, the loops move forward and catch the twig. *A Sea Snake*, from Murray Isle, in which the snake appears twisted round two parallel strings, and on slowly separating the hands he swims as the string unwinds. The *Setting Sun*, also from Murray Isle, in which the rayed sun slowly sinks below the horizon And lastly, *Tallow Dips*, an indigenous British figure, dealing with the misadventures of a thief who stole a bunch of candle-dips, was arrested, and finally hanged

More difficult, and in my opinion not well suited to beginners, are the following :—*The Fighting Lions*, from Bulawayo in East Africa, in which two loops representing lions alternately approach each other and then draw back, while the natives chant something representing the roaring of the lions. The *Head Hunters*, which, like so many of these designs, comes from Murray Isle. The construction leads to two twisted loops representing two warriors. On extending the hands the two men meet in the middle, and, on working the hands carefully, one loop breaks up, leaving only a kink representing the head of the defeated warrior. On continuing the extension, the victorious loop travels forward pushing in front of it the head of the victim. By making a knot in the string come into one of the twists we can make sure that that warrior shall be successful ; and this knowledge may be useful, since usually, before the game begins, the tribes from which the warriors come are mentioned—slimness in such matters is not confined to white men.   An *Alaskan River*, from British Columbia: this shows the course of a river, the appearance of a mosquito, and then a man fishing from a boat.

References for the workings of these additional figures are given under the heading, " Authorities."

Supplement: Openings and Typical Movements

[Pictures reproduced from Caroline Furness Jayne, *String Figures*, New York, Charles Scribner's Sons, 1906; reprinted by Dover Publications, Inc., as *String Figures and How to Make Them*, 1962. Text for First Position and Opening A is from Jayne; captions and text for other positions supplied by the editors.]

FIRST POSITION

First, Put the little fingers into the loop of string, and separate the hands.

You now have a single loop on each little finger passing directly and uncrossed to the opposite little finger.

Second, Turning the hands with the palms away from you, put each thumb into the little finger loop from below, and pick up on the back of the thumb the near little finger string; then, allowing the far little finger string to remain on the little finger, turn the hands with the palms facing each other, return the

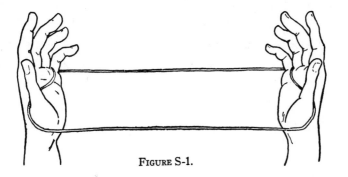

FIGURE S-1.

thumbs to their extended position, and draw the strings tight
(Fig. S-1).

In the First Position, therefore, there is, on each hand, a
string which crosses the palm, and passing behind the thumb
runs to the other hand to form the near thumb string of the
figure, and passing behind the little finger runs to the other
hand to form the far little finger string.

It is not essential that the loop shall be put on the hands by
the movements just described; any method will answer, so long
as the proper position of the string is secured.

OPENING A

First, Put the loop on the hands in the First Position.

Second, Bring the hands together, and put the right index up
under the string which crosses the left palm (Fig. S-2), and

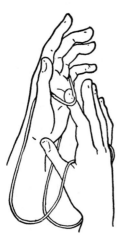

FIGURE S-2.

FIGURE S-3.

draw the loop out on the back of the finger by separating the hands.

Third, Bring the hands together again, and put the left index up under that part of the string crossing the palm of the right hand which is between the strings on the right index (Fig. S-3), and draw the loop out on the back of the left index by separating the hands.

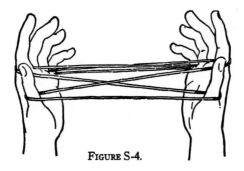

FIGURE S-4.

You now have a loop on each thumb, index, and little finger (Fig. S-4). There is a near thumb string and a far little finger string passing directly from one hand to the other, and two crosses formed between them by the near little finger string of one hand becoming the far index string of the other hand, and the far thumb string of one hand becoming the near index string of the other hand.

OPENING B

Opening B is exactly like Opening A except that the right palmar string is taken up by the left index finger before the left palmar string is taken up by the right index finger. See p. 21 of text and Figures S-5 and S-6.

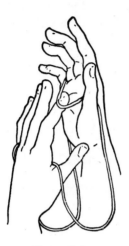

FIGURE S-5.

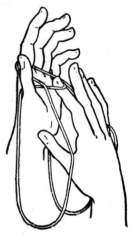

FIGURE S-6.

THE NAVAHO OPENING

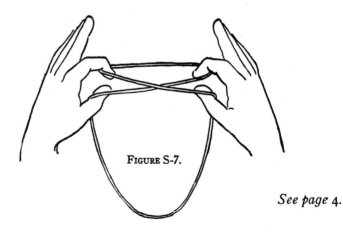

FIGURE S-7.

See page 4.

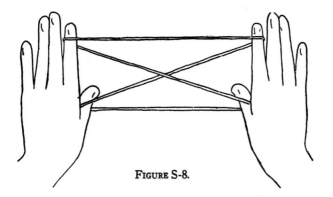

Figure S-8.

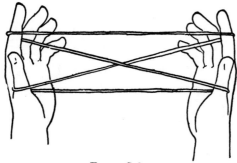

Figure S-9.

NAVAHOING A LOOP

See page 21.

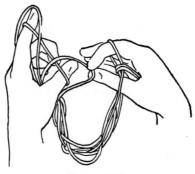

FIGURE S-10.

Authorities

The following notes give references to the sources from which the figures above described are taken. The excellent works by Jayne and Haddon, namely, "String Figures," by C. F. Jayne,* pp. xxiv. + 408, New York, 1906, and "Cat's Cradles from Many Lands," by K. Haddon, pp. xvi. + 96, London, 1911, mentioned in my Lecture, are more accessible than the articles in which the discoveries of these figures were first announced, and accordingly, when practicable, I refer, by choice, to these books (in which the sources of information are quoted) rather than to the original memoirs. Comparing the two authors, Jayne, like the present writer, uses, as far as may be, ordinary language, while Haddon is more concise, and following modern ethnologists, freely employs technical terms ; Jayne usually gives a diagram showing the positions of the hands and string after each step, while Haddon generally gives only the final arrangement of the string, not showing the hands.

1. *A Fish Spear* : see Jayne, p. 32, and Haddon, p. 7.

2. *An Outrigged Canoe* : see R. H. Compton, Journal of the Royal Anthropological Institute, vol. 49, p. 210, a paper excellent in form, and instructive alike to the novice and the expert.

3. *A Moth*: see Journal of the Royal Anthropological Institute, vol. xxxvi, p. 149.

4. *A Frame-Work for a Hut*: for this, as made in Central Africa, see W. A. Cunnington, Journal of the Royal Anthropological Institute, vol. xxxvi, p. 124, and Haddon, p. 29 ; and as made by the Red Indians, see Jayne, p. 243, and Haddon, p. 47.

5. *The Batoka Gorge* : see Haddon, p. 40.

6. *Carrying Wood* : see Jayne, p. 66, and Haddon, p. 46.

7. *A Tent Flap* : see Jayne, p. 12.

8. *Crow's Feet* : see Jayne, p. 116, and Haddon, p. 73.

9. *Lightning* : see Jayne, p. 216, Haddon, p. 51, and Compton, *loc. cit.* p. 232.

10. *Little Fishes* : see Jayne, p. 233, and Haddon, p. 12.

11. *The Veiled Sun* : see Jayne, p. 160, and Haddon, p. 32

---

* (Dover Reprint)

12. *A Fishing Net* : see Jayne, p. 24, and Haddon, p. 36. For a Net with two meshes see Double Diamonds, Jayne, p. 28, and for alternative constructions, Jayne, pp. 129, 228, 323. One mesh of a net can be made as shown in Jayne, pp. 64, 65, 391, 392. A way of making three meshes in line is given in my Salmon Net. In the Ebbing Tide we get successively 2, 4, 6, 8 meshes in line.

13. *A Butterfly* : see Jayne, p. 219.

14. *The Laia Fruit*: this was given to me by the discoverer.

15. *Cat's Cradle* : see my Mathematical Recreations, ninth edition, pp. 350-356, and Jayne, pp. 324-336.

16. Concerning other Figures in Class A mentioned above, for the history and working of *Double Diamonds*, see Jayne, p. 28; of *Two Chiefs*, see Jayne, p. 188 ; of a *Square*, see Jayne, p. 392 ; of a *Face-Mark*, see Haddon, p. 37 ; of *Many Stars*, see Jayne, p. 48, and Haddon, p. 50 ; and of *Circles and Triangles*, see Jayne, p. 146. For those of a *Rabbit*, see Jayne, p. 79 ; of a *Sea Gull*, see Haddon, p. 57 ; of *Two Elks*, see Jayne, p. 74 ; and of *Tree Burial*, see Rishbeth, Appendix to my Lecture as printed in the Proceedings of the Royal Institution, p. 98.

17. *The Mosquito*: this is a common pattern, for the working given above see F. E. Lutz, Anthropological Papers, Amer. Mus. of Nat. Hist., vol. xii., New York, 1912.

18. *A Siberian House* : see Haddon, p. 53.

19. *The Elusive Loop* : the construction given in the text has been common in England for more than half-a-century. A different design is given by Jayne, p. 352.

20. *Fluttering Wings*: see Haddon, p. 10.

21. *The Yam Thief* : this construction is widely known, see Man, 1902, pp. 141, 153 ; Jayne, p. 340, Haddon, p. 80, and Compton, *loc. cit.* p. 233.

22. *Throwing a Spear* : see Jayne, p. 131, and Haddon, p. 8.

23. *A Man Climbing a Tree* : see Haddon, p. 69.

24. *The Sleeper* . see Jayne, p. 192, and Haddon, p. 11.

25. *A Well* : see Jayne, p. 85, and Haddon, p. 17.

26. *A Fence* : see Jayne, p. 88, and Haddon, p. 19.

27. *A Salmon Net* : see Jayne, p. 142.

28. *The Caterpillar* : see Jayne, p. 253, and Compton, *loc. cit.* p. 228.

29. *The Ebbing Tide* : see Compton, *loc. cit.* p. 224, and for the Reversing Movement, Rishbeth in the Appendix to my Lecture, *loc cit.* pp. 101—2.

30. *The Porker* : see Compton, *loc. cit.* p. 229.

31. Concerning other Figures in Class B mentioned above, for the history and working of *Two Lads* : see Compton, *loc. cit.* p. 207 of *Two Eyes*, see Journal of the Royal Anthropological Institute, vol. xxxvi., p. 135, No. 7; of *Two Boys Fighting for an Arrow*, see Jayne, p. 317 ; of a *Sea Snake*, see Jayne, p. 34, and Haddon, p. 16 ; of the *Setting Sun*, see Jayne, p. 21, and Haddon, p. 24 ; and of *Tallow Dips*, see Jayne, p. 248, and Haddon, p. 74. For those of the *Fighting Lions*, see Journal of the Royal Anthropological Institute, vol. xxxvi., p. 146, and Haddon, p. 41 ; of the *Head Hunters*, see Jayne, p. 16, and Haddon, p. 22, and of an *Alaskan River*, see the Appendix to my Lecture, *loc. cit.* pp. 102—3.

32. I have not dealt in this paper with examples in Class Γ. Here, however, are ten examples with references, for any reader who may like to try them ; the *Lizard Twist*, see Jayne, p. 337, or Haddon, p. 80 ; the *Chippewa Release*, see Jayne, p. 346, or Haddon, p. 87 ; *Cheating the Halter*, see Jayne, p. 339, Haddon, p. 86, or R. H. Compton, *loc cit.* p. 234; the *Threading of a Closed Loop*, see Jayne, p. 354, or Haddon, p. 89 ; the *Fly on the Nose*, see Jayne, p. 348, or Haddon, p. 83; the *Joining the Ends of a Cut String*, see almost any book on easy conjuring or parlour tricks, for instance, Hoffmann's Modern Magic, p. 317 ; the *Interlaced Handcuffs or Fetters*, see Hoffmann's Puzzles, p. 349 ; the *Button Hole Trick* (otherwise worked with a key or ring threaded on a closed loop), see Tom Tit's Scientific Amusements, London, 1919, p. 404 ; the *Knife in the Tree*, Ibid, 399 ; and the *Reversed Twist*, Ibid, p. 400.

Index and Glossary

The Index includes a Glossary of the terms in common use.

Ulnar: of two strings held on the hand that on the little-finger side of the hand is called ulnar. When the hands are held in the normal position this is the far string.   *See* pp. 10, 23

Uprooting the Alou, 49, 50
Uvean Figure, 61

Vancouver Figure, 16
Veiled Sun, 35, 36

Well, 53, 54
Wings, Fluttering, 48, 49

Yam Thief 7, 49, 50
Yoruba Figures, 55, 64

Zambesi Figure, 15, 29
Zulu Figure, 26

A CATALOG OF SELECTED
DOVER BOOKS
IN ALL FIELDS OF INTEREST

A CATALOG OF SELECTED DOVER
BOOKS IN ALL FIELDS OF INTEREST

THE ART NOUVEAU STYLE, edited by Roberta Waddell. 579 rare photographs of works in jewelry, metalwork, glass, ceramics, textiles, architecture and furniture by 175 artists—Mucha, Seguy, Lalique, Tiffany, many others. 288pp. 8⅜ × 11¼.
23515-7 Pa. $9.95

AMERICAN COUNTRY HOUSES OF THE GILDED AGE (Sheldon's "Artistic Country-Seats"), A. Lewis. All of Sheldon's fascinating and historically important photographs and plans. New text by Arnold Lewis. Approx. 200 illustrations. 128pp. 9⅜ × 12¼.
24301-X Pa. $7.95

THE WAY WE LIVE NOW, Anthony Trollope. Trollope's late masterpiece, marks shift to bitter satire. Character Melmotte "his greatest villain." Reproduced from original edition with 40 illustrations. 416pp. 6⅛ × 9¼.
24360-5 Pa. $7.95

BENCHLEY LOST AND FOUND, Robert Benchley. Finest humor from early 30's, about pet peeves, child psychologists, post office and others. Mostly unavailable elsewhere. 73 illustrations by Peter Arno and others. 183pp. 5⅜ × 8½.
22410-4 Pa. $3.50

ISOMETRIC PERSPECTIVE DESIGNS AND HOW TO CREATE THEM, John Locke. Isometric perspective is the picture of an object adrift in imaginary space. 75 mindboggling designs. 52pp. 8¼ × 11.
24123-8 Pa. $2.75

PERSPECTIVE FOR ARTISTS, Rex Vicat Cole. Depth, perspective of sky and sea, shadows, much more, not usually covered. 391 diagrams, 81 reproductions of drawings and paintings. 279pp. 5⅜ × 8½.
22487-2 Pa. $4.00

MOVIE-STAR PORTRAITS OF THE FORTIES, edited by John Kobal. 163 glamor, studio photos of 106 stars of the 1940s: Rita Hayworth, Ava Gardner, Marlon Brando, Clark Gable, many more. 176pp. 8⅜ × 11¼.
23546-7 Pa. $6.95

STARS OF THE BROADWAY STAGE, 1940-1967, Fred Fehl. Marlon Brando, Uta Hagen, John Kerr, John Gielgud, Jessica Tandy in great shows—*South Pacific, Galileo, West Side Story*, more. 240 black-and-white photos. 144pp. 8⅜ × 11¼.
24398-2 Pa. $8.95

ILLUSTRATED DICTIONARY OF HISTORIC ARCHITECTURE, edited by Cyril M. Harris. Extraordinary compendium of clear, concise definitions for over 5000 important architectural terms complemented by over 2000 line drawings. 592pp. 7½ × 9⅜.
24444-X Pa. $14.95

THE EARLY WORK OF FRANK LLOYD WRIGHT, F.L. Wright. 207 rare photos of Oak Park period, first great buildings: Unity Temple, Dana house, Larkin factory. Complete photos of Wasmuth edition. New Introduction. 160pp. 8⅜ × 11¼.
24381-8 Pa. $7.95

LIVING MY LIFE, Emma Goldman. Candid, no holds barred account by foremost American anarchist: her own life, anarchist movement, famous contemporaries, ideas and their impact. 944pp. 5⅜ × 8½. 22543-7, 22544-5 Pa., Two-vol. set $13.00

UNDERSTANDING THERMODYNAMICS, H.C. Van Ness. Clear, lucid treatment of first and second laws of thermodynamics. Excellent supplement to basic textbook in undergraduate science or engineering class. 103pp. 5⅜ × 8.
63277-6 Pa. $5.50

THE PRINCIPLE OF RELATIVITY, Albert Einstein et al. Eleven most important original papers on special and general theories. Seven by Einstein, two by Lorentz, one each by Minkowski and Weyl. 216pp. 5⅜ × 8½. 60081-5 Pa. $4.00

PINEAPPLE CROCHET DESIGNS, edited by Rita Weiss. The most popular crochet design. Choose from doilies, luncheon sets, bedspreads, apron—34 in all. 32 photographs. 48pp. 8¼ × 11. 23939-X Pa. $2.00

REPEATS AND BORDERS IRON-ON TRANSFER PATTERNS, edited by Rita Weiss. Lovely florals, geometrics, fruits, animals, Art Nouveau, Art Deco and more. 48pp. 8¼ × 11. 23428-2 Pa. $1.95

SCIENCE-FICTION AND HORROR MOVIE POSTERS IN FULL COLOR, edited by Alan Adler. Large, full-color posters for 46 films including *King Kong, Godzilla, The Illustrated Man,* and more. A bug-eyed bonanza of scantily clad women, monsters and assorted other creatures. 48pp. 10¼ × 14¼. 23452-5 Pa. $8.95

TECHNICAL MANUAL AND DICTIONARY OF CLASSICAL BALLET, Gail Grant. Defines, explains, comments on steps, movements, poses and concepts. 15-page pictorial section. Basic book for student, viewer. 127pp. 5⅜ × 8½. 21843-0 Pa. $2.95

STORYBOOK MAZES, Dave Phillips. 23 stories and mazes on two-page spreads: *Wizard of Oz, Treasure Island, Robin Hood,* etc. Solutions. 64pp. 8¼ × 11. 23628-5 Pa. $2.25

PUNCH-OUT PUZZLE KIT, K. Fulves. Engaging, self-contained space age entertainments. Ready-to-use pieces, diagrams, detailed solutions. Challenge a robot, split the atom, more. 40pp. 8¼ × 11. 24307-9 Pa. $3.50

THE HUMAN FIGURE IN MOTION, Eadweard Muybridge. Over 4500 19th-century photos showing stopped-action sequences of undraped men, women, children jumping, running, sitting, other actions. Monumental collection. 390pp. 7⅞ × 10⅝. 20204-6 Clothbd. $18.95

PHOTOGRAPHIC SKETCHBOOK OF THE CIVIL WAR, Alexander Gardner. Reproduction of 1866 volume with 100 on-the-field photographs: Manassas, Lincoln on battlefield, slave pens, etc. 224pp. 10⅝ × 8¼. 22731-6 Pa. $7.95

FLORAL IRON-ON TRANSFER PATTERNS, edited by Rita Weiss. 55 floral designs, large and small, realistic, stylized; poppies, iris, roses, etc. Victorian, modern. Instructions. 48pp. 8¼ × 11. 23248-4 Pa. $1.95

AUTOBIOGRAPHY: The Story of My Experiments with Truth, Mohandas K. Gandhi. Boyhood, legal studies, purification, the growth of the Satyagraha (nonviolent protest) movement. Critical, inspiring work of the man who freed India. 480pp. 5⅜ × 8½. 24593-4 Pa. $6.95

ON THE IMPROVEMENT OF THE UNDERSTANDING, Benedict Spinoza. Also contains *Ethics, Correspondence,* all in excellent R Elwes translation. Basic works on entry to philosophy, pantheism, exchange of ideas with great contemporaries. 420pp. 5⅜ × 8½. 20250-X Pa. $5.95

Prices subject to change without notice.

Available at your book dealer or write for free catalog to Dept. GI, Dover Publications, Inc., 31 East 2nd St. Mineola, N.Y. 11501. Dover publishes more than 175 books each year on science, elementary and advanced mathematics, biology, music, art, literary history, social sciences and other areas.